MUSINGS
M for OM

MUSINGS
MOM for

NICOLE MERRITT

This book is dedicated to Josh, Payton, Weston and Harper—I love you more. And, yes, it is possible.

CONTENTS

WELCOME

To motherhood.

To this wacky ride.

To an adventure in self-discovery like no other.

Or maybe this isn't your first rodeo.

Perhaps you're a seasoned mama,
a mama to bigs, or an empty nester.

Regardless…I'm happy you're here.

And I hope that, generally, you're happy.

To be a mother.

To be a woman.

To be someone's partner, perhaps.

But as it may be, you might not be happy all the time.

Conceivably, motherhood is hard on you.

Motherhood has or is changing you.

And maybe, like me, you've come to realize
that as you're putting in Goliath-sized effort tending to,

teaching, and raising your love nuggets,

motherhood and marriage raise you—
whether you like it or not.

And you won't always like it.

But sometimes, you'll really love it.

It's a wild journey, my dear friends,
and without a doubt, you are cut out for it.

But if ever you question your capabilities or strength,

lean into this book and its reminders and let it rouse you
to what a total badass of a woman you are.

I hope you enjoy these ramblings as much
as I enjoy having you to share them with.

PATIENCE

Let's start with this one because Lord knows
you're going to need an abundance of it.

With yourself, your kids, your spouse,
and the general judgy public,

Patience is a virtue that not very many people have.

Me? Guilty. Mine is scarce. Perhaps yourself included?

And here's the annoying thing about patience: when we need
it the most, it's typically nowhere to be found…just like a
mama who has completely lost all of hers.

I know where you can find her, though:

crying in a bathroom or the shower,

eating chocolate in her closet, in the drive-through line
as she waits for McDonald's,

driving aimlessly in her car, blaring either some
God music or some very ungodly rap,

or attempting to find some calm and/or a laugh by ignoring
anything (and anyone) that might pull her away from the
lovely escape that is her disregarding her surroundings and
immersing herself in social media feeds.

Listen…

It's OK to tap or tune out sometimes.

It's OK to lose your cool.

And it's OK to blow your lid.

So long as you find that fudger and put it back on, ya know?

Motherhood is hard, and it takes the cake when
it comes to pushing a human to their limits.

You're going to feel on top of it all and in control
one minute and like you're drowning the next.

Sometimes you'll wanna call for help, while other times you'll
lack the energy or desire to send out any sort of SOS.

Be patient with yourself,

be kind to yourself,

and honor your emotions by feeling all the feels.

Then be patient with your kids, kind to them, too,
and honor their emotions by allowing them to feel
and live in their feelings whenever they need.

Do the same for your spouse,
which won't be easy, but it's important.

And when it comes to the general judgy public,

as hard as it will be, and it will be hard, have patience
with them. You never know if today was a day they lost
theirs, and with it, their way.

Finally, if you've made it to this point,
I thank you for your patience with me as I get
to the focal point of the topic, which is—

you've got to have patience with the
process of finding more patience.

Take me, for example...

I'm on year thirty-five of my life and year ten of being a
parent, and I still lose my shiitake multiple times a day.

Because

life,

mothering,

wife-ing,

and woman-ing be like that.

You know that Rome wasn't built in a day,
so it shouldn't come as a surprise that

a patient demeanor isn't either.

Still, you've got to lay the bricks or, at minimum, have a plan
for finding and laying them, or you'll never have one.

So take it

one brick at a time,

one moment at a time,

one kid at a time,

one conversation at a time,

one day at a time,

and you'll get there.

(I'm hoping I will too.)

GRACE

Let me introduce you to "grace."

She's your new best friend.

Whether you like it or not, and whether or not you're
looking to add to your support system arsenal,

you and I need her.

And, yes, grace is a her because, by definition, it means
"courteous goodwill," and, well, that's pretty much what we
mothers try to exude, all day e'r' day on end.

Us mamas know firsthand how it helps a family
stay connected by (at least attempting to) exude a

friendly, helpful, and cooperative attitude, unconditionally.

The problem?

That sometimes, we fall into the trap that is

extending grace to others and not ourselves

or, occasionally,

to ourselves but not to others.

So here's what we've got to do…keep grace
in our back pocket and whip her out whenever the heck
a situation feels tense, uncomfortable, confusing, scary,
or irritating. So pretty much all the time.

Let's look to grace and ask her to help
us accept situations, conversations, and people

we might otherwise have a hard time
welcoming and riding out.

And if ever we question if we're made out for motherhood,
marriage, our job or a particular task, let's remember what
grace guides us to do, which is to ask ourselves,

"Are you ready to evolve?"

That answer? It's always *yes*.

BOUNDARIES

They're not just for sports fields anymore.

They are hard to establish, hard to keep,
but extremely necessary.

If you want to keep any semblance of peace,

if you're going to raise mentally healthy, respectful children,

if you want a fulfilling marriage or relationship,

then you need boundaries…

Though even just the word sounds negative, right?

"A dividing line" does not scream, "Let's come together."

So naturally, setting a or many boundaries feels like
you are creating separation, not connection.

But here's another way to look at it…

Think of yourself as setting boundaries because you
love people (and pretty frankly yourself too)
and not as a sign that you don't.

When I draw a line in the sand when it comes to sharing my
energy, attention, time, money, opinion,

or presence, it's saying,

"I notice I'm feeling a bit depleted, frustrated, or discouraged, and I want to feel better—for you, for me, and for my level of productivity, and so I'm setting these boundaries to protect the both of us because that's who I care about."

Setting boundaries is also a way of helping younger humans, like your children, become more responsible.

All that being said, if I could set a better boundary between myself and the fridge, it would really help with my mom bod.

PERFECTIONISM

It's such a waste.

Of your time.

Of your energy.

So *stop*.

Let it go.

Pull a full-on Elsa, and anytime you start to feel flawed
or less than "perfect" and see that as your irreparable defect,
freeze that negative and irrational thought and walk away
from it. Or rather, confidently storm away. From it and from
any self-worth and confidence-attacking thoughts that leave
you feeling like somehow you're

not "enough."

What does that even mean to "be enough"?

The only thing you have to be enough of…is your dang self.

Your authentic, überunique, gorgeous, empowered,
talented, and wholly capable self.

That fascination and addiction to desiring to look, sound,
and be "perfect," it's "top dog syndrome," a made-up

syndrome that I have suffered from my whole life.

The cure?

Coming to terms and aligning all your thinking
with the belief that

there is no top and bottom, best and worst,
or only winners and failures.

There's just a messy middle where we all reside,
and really it's quite special there.

Some filter our middle, making our lives
and selves appear more attractive to others,

while others sugarcoat theirs,
only showing to the world the sweeter bits.

You don't do either. 'Cause you don't need to be perfect.

Do you know what you do need to do, though?
It's relish in the fact that you are perfectly you
and that you are doing a perfectly fine job working
to gradually improve upon who that is.

I'm impressed by you.
And it would serve you well if you were too.

CONFUSION

Be prepared to operate in a steady state of being eternally perplexed by situations, people, and even your feelings.

It's a good thing, though. It forces introspection, growth, and situational and social awareness.

I know this constant uncertainty feels uncomfortable, but you've got to get comfortable with feeling regularly anxious and addled.

Why?

Because perhaps the most poignant feature of motherhood is its propensity to both disorient, then reorient the dear woman living through it.

It'll rattle your cage.

It'll make you want to stay in one.

It'll scare you.

But you don't scare easily.

You're a beautiful, powerful, and proficient beast, and you've got nothing to be scared of.

LOSING IT

Your mind,

patience,

sanity,

car keys,

your phone,

who you were,

your hobbies,

your once closer-to-perfect body,

friends,

relationships,

your time,

energy,

and mental stability.

Say sayonara to it all.

But say hello to

learning about strengths you didn't know you had,

coping with change,

becoming a pro at adapting,

and impressing yourself more than you ever thought possible.

JUDGY PEEPS

Are.

Everywhere.

But hear this—

so is the glitter you choose to sprinkle all over this world
and its unsuspecting beings via your

honest nature,

genuine smile,

and unconditional compassion.

If someone wants to judge you,

and many will,

let 'em.

Just don't return the favor and do it back.

Keep cognizant that people who judge likely feel
and suffer the pain of having been judged.

Be a remedy for them;

douse them with your kindness and unwillingness

to engage in any sort of negativity.

And perhaps, your lack of improper reaction
will show them how to be, which is kind, always.

FRIENDSHIPS

They aren't as uncomplicated as when you were a kid, and it'll feel like you have a lot less time for them.

You'll make some friends.

You'll lose some friends.

Some friendships will last a while, and some, well, they will be fun while they last.

Here's what they shouldn't be:

Challenging.

Lots of work.

A source of stress.

Anxiety inducing.

Restrictive.

Demanding.

Fake.

Here's what they should be:

Easy.

Enjoyable.

Convenient.

Relaxed.

Safe.

Fulfilling.

Peace inciting.

Accepting.

Authentic.

And you know what's fantastic about friendships, even those that come and go? It's that every one of 'em changes you, and that's pretty neat.

INSECURITY

Mine's got me questioning if you're enjoying this book.

It also makes me wonder if I'm "qualified" to write one.

It's got me pondering if you think

I've got a big nose,

are questioning where my eyebrows have gone,

or are baffled by the fact that I think I can write
and that my stories are worth being told.

It also makes me feel like I'm getting nothing right,
and perhaps yours makes you feel the same.

Be it about your

body,

career,

marriage,

or you as a mother, daughter, sister, or friend,

unhealthy thoughts creep in and weigh on you.

Release the thoughts.

Loosen the grip they have on you and you on them.

And if ever they make you feel like crawling into your

less-than-stunning,

obviously aging,

unconfident shell at times.

Don't.

Wear your mistake-making, self-questioning humanness
like a badge of freakin' incredible honor.

What a gift you are to this world as a soul-housing being,

raising one or more heart happy humans

as you each try to share who you are with this world

—in your unique way, of course—

intending and hoping to leave a positive mark on it.

You've got nothing to be insecure about when you
are secure with the fact that your worth is undeniably
inherent and does not need to be earned.

VILLAGES

They are great to have—that's for sure.

They step in when you need to step out.

They step up when you're dying to step down (for an
extended period or even for just for a moment).

They linger when you ask them to "please stay longer."

They leave (and are unoffended) when it's clear
that's what you desire.

Villages rock.

But honestly, you don't need one.

Because you, my gorgeous friend, are a village
and a rock all on your lonesome.

Help is excellent, and you should never hesitate to ask for
some—from family, friends, or whomever.

But be sure of this, too, the big guy in the sky,

he'll always help you if you call out to him.

Even if

you're not religious.

Even if you're

"not that into Jesus."

Even if you don't believe in him,

please know there are so many people,
worldly and heavenly, who believe in *you*.

*A*WAKENED

To what a blessing your one life is.

To all that matters.

To all that you are.

Some days you will feel it, and some days you won't.

One undeniable truth?

Your kid(s) will forever turn you "on" to the incredible honor
that is getting to share your life with them.

And do you know what else?

They'll constantly force you to change channels,
and thank God for that because the best thing
for us imperfect beings is metamorphosis.

As I'm sure you are well aware,

being fully and wholly thankful for and engaged in your
daily life and the things and people that make it up,

it's not easy.

It happens gradually, and if you're lucky,
you get better at it every day.

Appreciate the process,

be an active participant in it,

and always remember a new

second,

minute,

hour,

and day are on the horizon.

Stay tuned because great things are ahead for you.

FORGIVENESS

This is a big one, ladies.

Let's start getting comfortable forgiving ourselves.

For being

"a lot,"

"not enough,"

"too much,"

or "too little."

For not sooner realizing that we never have to apologize
for any of that ish in the first place.

Let's also get comfortable forgiving others,
like those who have wronged us.

Because holding on to that pain and those grudges,
it serves no purpose.

While we expect that not forgiving another is armor that can
protect us from them inflicting any future hurt upon us, it
sadly isn't and can't prevent that.

All anger really does is act like quicksand—pulling us deeper

into our discomfort and dismay and
making it harder for us to escape it.

And so I feel it bears repeating that though we often see
forgiveness as benefiting the wrongdoer, the truth is that
absolution is much more advantageous for the one who was
wronged than it will ever be for the one who caused the hurt.

MARRIAGE

Oh boy.

What to say about this?

Especially when you're married to one.

A grown one who tells dad jokes.

Who isn't chompin' at the bit to

do the cooking,

load the dishwasher,

or

fold the laundry.

Marriage.

It isn't always joyous.

And that's totally normal.

(Thank God.)

Let's lead with that—the fact that your marriage isn't
and will never be "perfect."

But…

if you choose the right person, it mostly will be.

Not every minute, hour, day, or week,
but in big-picture, life-together terms,

it mostly will be.

There will be seasons, no doubt, the fruitful kind
and the depleting kind.

There will be a lot of ebbing and flowing when it comes to

what you need from and how you feel about one another.

But at its crux

(or foundation, depending upon how you want
to look at your partnership) is

two people who care a ridiculous hell of a lot
about one another and enough to stick together
despite any of the bullsh*t they face.

And there's a lot of shiitake that you'll both face.

Perhaps as you're reading this, you're
living through some of that ish.

So what you do is this:

you ask yourself,

today and every married day that follows,

"Is there enough good stuff here in this space for me to see myself living like this with this particular imperfect human for the rest of my days or, at minimum, the extended future?"

If the answer is yes, you keep on the coaster.

If the answer is no, then you unbuckle
and you brace for a fallout,

fully aware that your support system
will be right there to catch you.

Solitude

What even is that?

"The state of being alone."

The concept will seem so foreign to you once you have kids.

And though you'll rarely have any of it once
you become a mom,

oddly enough,

if ever you get some

—if you're anything like me—

you struggle with

how to spend it,

feel an immense amount of guilt for it,

miss your kids,

and then miss and complain that you don't
get enough of it once it's gone.

Welcome to the merry-go-round that is
the emotional carousel known as motherhood,

where the flip-flopping of your feelings
and head spinning never stops.

Now hold on and,

dare I say,

try to enjoy the crazy-making ride.

'Cause goodness knows, when it's over, you're going to miss it
and not your solitude.

TIME

When you're young, you think there's an infinite amount.

You think you have all the time in the world, and be damned anyone who tries to tell you othewise.

That's until you start having kids and creating a family of your very own, and then, poof! It's gone.

All that time you thought you had, and suddenly, well, now there's never enough of it.

Never enough time to get everything done on your to-do list.

Never enough alone time with your spouse.

Never enough time with your little kids before

(in what seems like a very looooong blink)

they are big kids.

Never enough time to (successfully) chase each and every dream you've got.

There's never enough time for any of that.

And surely not enough time to

serve up Pinterest-worthy meals,

get to the gym,

get together with girlfriends,

or wash, fold, *and* put away a load of laundry
all on the same day.

There's never enough time.

Or is there?

There's this truth we mamas often hide from ourselves, which
is that there is time enough to ask ourselves,

"Am I doing enough with the time I've got?"

Because perhaps there is enough time for some of this, in
pockets, of course.

And on any given day, it's up to each of us to decide what to
put in or do with those pockets of time.

And only you, alone, can be certain that you are doing
enough with your time.

And not "enough" as is in

productivity and visible output

but as in a soul-satisfying,
filling-your-internal-bucket-full sort of way.

Make time for that sh*t, please, because it's super important.

WORK

Should you or shouldn't you have a job
beyond mothering your children?

Or maybe you don't have the choice or the luxury
to stay at home with them.

If you work outside of the home,

you're praised for providing for your family and

not foregoing a career in the name of old-fashioned
domestication.

But you're also

touted as selfish,

often labeled a "hands-off parent"

and seen as valuing money and status over your children.

If you don't "work" but still totally work inside of your home
as a stay-at-home momma, you are praised for

putting family first,

valuing how your children are mentally
and emotionally provided for, and

deemed selfless for martyring your career dreams in the name
of your ten-fingered, ten-toed living ones.

But you're also labeled

lazy,

a moocher off your spouse,

unmotivated,

and unwilling to assign yourself more than one role,
perhaps because you're scared?

So they insinuate.

You can't win here, ladies.

When it comes to the general public, whether you work

inside of your nuclear walls or outside
of that lovingly chaotic psych ward

or both, or any combination of the above,

somebody, or even more than likely, many somebodies, is
going to take issue with and have words to say about it.

And I'm betting it isn't going to be positive,
kind, or make you feel good.

Screw them.

No, really. I mean that.

In the

nicest,

most Christian,

least potty-mouthed way,

screw them.

I mean it enough to say it twice, but I'll only say this once
because I know you're going to agree:

your decision on how to provide for your family and how to
spend your days is nobody's business but your own.

Because with your one life,

you should be in the business of pleasing no one
but your damn self and soul.

Everyone else, well, they can namaste out of your business.

In It for the Laughs

You've just got to be.

You've got to resign yourself to the fact that this transformation-prompting life of yours and motherhood are going to break you into a million pieces and bring you to your knees.

Those callus knees from which you'll find yourself praying.

But where I beg and plead, you also find yourself laughing.

To laugh at our mistakes is to take back what those mistakes took from us,

like our confidence, and we need that.

Like a plant needs sunlight and water, you and I need humor and more humor to ride out our often uncomfortable and painful but certainly beautiful growth.

GRATITUDE

It's your best ally against

anxiety,

despair,

loneliness,

and frustration.

But an "attitude of gratitude" is also
the hardest thing to keep.

"You just tore this room that I just cleaned to shreds!"

(But I'm grateful for you, you little maniac three-year-old.)

"The dinner just spilled everywhere because you left your
shoes in the middle of the kitchen and ran off!"

(But I'm still grateful for you and the ability
to put food on the table, of course

[or, in this case, the floor].)

I'm just so very grateful and, of course, #blessed.

(Insert eye roll here.)

(Insert palm to the face here.)

Because gratitude is a flippin' challenge to stay on top of.

Because speaking of "on top of,"
that's what everyone is to Mom:

up her biscuit and at every turn around the corner.

It's exhausting.

And so I complain and complain and complain,
and maybe you do too.

Until we realize and remember that if our present life
drastically changed tomorrow, or our dear loved ones were to
be taken from us, we wouldn't be able to go on.

We need everything and everyone in this life that drives us
crazy, and that stark acknowledgment and our consistent
awareness of such is what enables us to stay closer to
gratitude daily.

Being grateful doesn't mean you can't

complain,

worry,

or ever feel peeved by things,

but what it does is bring to the center of your attention what
and who matters most; and when you're laser focused on that,
the grumbles begin to dwindle.

MISTAKES

Holy hell, they are going to happen.

In droves.

You're gonna make them.

Your spouse is going to make them.

The kids are going to make a ton.

It's how each of you bounces back from them that's critical.

It's how you support each other in spite of and through them.

You know, it's not a horrible thing to screw up
in front of others.

Intentional or not, it's actually super brave
to own your flawed-ness.

When I see somebody who's not perfect, I'm not like

"Damn! Why ain't they acting perfect???"

Nope. Much to the contrary. I'm like

"Damn! This is good to see. Good to see
that I'm not the only one struggling."

Because here's what I think…

even more powerful than the fact that we are a world and community of fumblers who are "in this together" is that each of us is capable of redeeming ourselves and each has the capacity to aid and forgive each other.

A mistake doesn't define you; nor does the sum of yours.

What will forever define you, me, every one of us,

is how we

move past out mistakes,

move on,

and move forward toward being a slightly better human

in the next

minute,

hour,

day,

or year.

As a reformed perfectionist, I used to internally berate myself for my missteps.

Now,

slightly older and a tiny bit more enlightened,

I appreciate them.

Perhaps not in the exact moment when I'm in the thick of it or even in the very immediate aftermath, but post-gaffe,

I'm ultimately grateful for my error because without it,

I'd lack the lesson it brought with it.

Think of life like a video game, and when your character screws up, you lose a life but return to the same situation with new knowledge on what not to do so you can move forward and succeed—our mistakes do the same for us here in the real world.

THE LONG GAME

I stink at paying attention to this, and maybe you do too.

As mothers, we are so often consumed by the
"here and now."

This one test (is so important).

This one situation (is so dire).

This one thing that didn't go according to our best-laid plan
(will ruin the whole day).

Today's mistakes mean I am a horrible parent
(always have been and always will be).

We are so dramatic (though it is still entirely unacceptable for
our spouses, kids, or anyone else to remark such).

It's true—we totally can be, and the above
everyday thinking is proof of such.

Really, though, the only thing that needs your attention in the
immediate present is this mama (you) and this child/children
(your child/children).

Your short game?

It should only be that,

at your core,

you and them (and your spouse if you have one)

feel innately worthy and as close to "at peace" and hopeful as you can on any given day.

The short game cannot be focused on there being

100 percent good behavior (yours and theirs),

plans that always work out,

people that are always nice to you and yours,

or everything going the way you want.

While all that sounds well and good and ideal, it's just not realistic, at least not consistently.

When you change your perspective,

you can align your short game with a "win" being you

not just surviving your days and the inevitable curveballs, but living and appreciating them with a wholehearted, calm-centered, "I'm focused on keeping my peace" mind-set.

TRUST

In God or whoever/whatever that higher power is for you.

Trust yourself.

That you know what is and isn't for you.

Trust your village and that they will catch you if ever you need them to.

Trust how life is unfolding.

Trust in people.

That's a big one, folks, and often a challenging one.

And trust in how you are generally evolving as a human and specifically inside of the roles you hold.

One thing that I don't want you to place your trust in is

anyone,

any book,

any article,

or any advice that you should quit anything you enjoy or have a passion for.

Me?

I have a passion for eternally improving upon who I am and
sharing my journey with others.

Please believe me when I tell you that
you should share yours because,

without a doubt,

someone somewhere needs to hear your story
to help make sense of theirs.

MISSED OPPORTUNITIES

There will be what feels like a million of these whether you are a parent or not, but especially if you are, and if you're reading this book, I assume that's the case.

Let me make this clear:

You haven't, and you're not missing anything.

At least anything that's meant for you, that is.

Anything that is your fate, if you believe in that kind of stuff, which in a totally not crazy sort of way, I do.

Where you are in life at any moment is exactly where you are meant to be.

So enjoy *today's* opportunities—this is why you are alive—

For.

Every.

Single.

Today.

TREASURES

They're not just for pirates, and the best kind aren't found at the bottom of an ocean or buried inside a hidden temple.

The most precious treasure on this earth

was once inside you

and—now and forever—

always a part of you.

It's your children.

Value them.

The "whole person" them.

Value them more than anything in this entire world.

And if you can remember not to, don't waste another minute of your life pining for material things beyond them.

YOUR CUP

It runneth over with responsibilities,

leaving you feeling empty but at the same time full of

anxiety,

demands,

and expectations.

And how does an anxious, overfilled-on-the-outside-but-empty-on-the-inside cup feel?

Sh*tty.

Not all the time but sometimes, right?

And depleted of

energy,

motivation,

strength,

and appreciation.

Yes, you are the cup, so here's what you have to do…

Give that cup of yours a "no overfill" and a "no underfill"
line and stay the heck in the generally comfortable middle.

Speaking of the middle, that's where
you should fill your kids' cups to, as well.

Sure, there are very many occasions when filling their joy cup
to an overflow is warranted.

But I also dare suggest that to raise

well-rounded,

appropriately attached,

and successfully independent children,

we must leave and allow room for them to fill their cup full
by themselves. That way, they will know never to depend on
others or a single other to do that for them.

The world is "on tap."

Don't stay thirsty for more and
let what you get make you drunk.

Stay tranquil, and do that by knowing
the fill level you need on any given day.

FEELING LIKE A FAKE

Like me, sitting here as I write this book on motherhood and

"appreciating all the moments"

and remembering

"they're only little for so long"

on the heels of yelling at my three kids for the umpteenth time today because I'm incredibly tired of playing referee between the three siblings.

If you can go eighteen years without ever feeling like a fake or fraud or hypocrite, you're a magical unicorn.

But if you're not one of those and you're one of these—an average ridiculously imperfect human—you're going to have times where you feel like an imposter.

Here's how you combat that:

When the weather permits, open the windows.

You will inevitably forget that the windows are, in fact, open.

This will happen often.

You're "true" easily riled, semi-off-your-rocker self will

appear, loud enough for the neighbors to hear,
and your're prim and proper facade will no longer hold up.

They will hear you. They may now fear you.

But at least now they know you, the real you that is.

The you who doesn't mean to act like a witch but,
with what feels like the world's weight on her,
occasionally rides the broom.

She's not fake. She's just trying to be a better human and get
more of life and mothering right but still screwing up a lot.

That's not something to be embarrassed about or anything
to hide. It's authenticity, and, if nothing else, at least it's
respectably honest, and you're keepin' it real.

WRINKLES

In your schedule, day, and plan.

On your legs and your face.

In your marriage.

Wrinkles, wrinkles everywhere,
wrinkles, wrinkles, they don't care.

They are going to pop up and ruin your day whenever they
see fit, and there sure are plenty of reasons to despise them.

To be annoyed by them.

To think they make your

days,

life,

and you as a being less than beautiful.

But dang it, you're mistaken.

I have plenty of days where my plans and expectations, both
for myself and my kids, go to heck.

And, if we're talking forehead wrinkles, I have *at least* seven.

That's two for each kid I've got and one for the hubs.

These wrinkles on my face, partially due to all the wrinkles in my days, might make me look old, sure, but they also make old this…the idea that wrinkles are bad and we should do away with them.

I want to keep my face, booty, and day wrinkles because the latter force me to live and learn, and the first two are proof that I am.

HUMOR

It.

Will.

Help.

More than you think.

Probably more than you care to admit.

Unless it's your husband's

(or maybe just mine), and then it's annoying AF.

Just kidding.

But seriously, if you keep yours about you,
it'll be a terrific ally.

I recommend a high dose of humor, multiple times, daily.

And here's what side effects it may bring on:

a disappearance of your resting B face,

an unclenched jaw,

less yelling,

less crying,

and more laughter.

Holy heck, you should overdose on this stuff!

The best thing about it?

You don't need a prescription for it,

and you can keep it in a handy-dandy place—

right there in your back pocket.

Now pull that booger out whenever you need it
(and when you think you don't).

TONE

You have got to watch yours.

If you are anything like me, it will get you into trouble.

With your kids,

your spouse,

the general public,

even those people on the web who can pick up tone on an internet comment.

Who even knew that was possible?

And speaking of internet comments, don't ever leave 'em unless they are nice.

We learned this ish in kindergarten, remember?

If you can't say anything nice, don't say anything at all.

But let's add this—

that if and when you're going to say something, watch your delivery.

If you are going to say something, say it without a freakin' tone.

But that's only if you can figure out how to reign yours in.

Me? I haven't been that lucky.

I don't always struggle with keeping a calm, balanced persona and tranquil voice about me (yes, I do), but when I do (which is always), you can be sure it'll be in front of and directed at the people I love and need the most—my family.

I don't struggle with my delivery speed because I'm the reactive and rapid-response-firing type (you're welcome), but I am regularly challenged trying to speak without a crap ton of pent-up, raised emotion and releasing that semi-incoherent nonsense on the unsuspecting.

It isn't a great trait of mine, and I'm working on it, and if this sounds anything like you, maybe you can work on yours too.

Besides watching yours, do you know what else you've got to do when it comes to tones?

Don't pick up on other people's.

Because, at times, they aren't there; we've fabricated them.

And even if you are met with a clear and apparent tone-doused conversation, do your best not to pick it up.

Leave it with its owner,

where it belongs,

where it should stay so it can be worked on.

Please don't take it with you.

Take their words without the unkind way they came out,

take the underlying message,

but chalk up another's less-than-respectful-and-kind delivery
as an

"Oh well, we've all been there. I'm gonna hear what I think
you're saying sans your attitude
and not let your negative one affect mine."

It isn't easy, folks, but wouldn't you rather be tone-deaf
than constantly bombarded by unproductive noise?

I think I would.

MINDFULNESS

I love the idea of it.

I know many people that "practice" it.

I just can't do it.

And when I say "it," I mean that I don't

meditate,

do yoga,

know what chakras are and how to align mine.

I kind of loathe solitude, and too much quiet makes me
uncomfortable (and bored).

But here's the thing—

none of those things actually constitutes mindfulness.

They are pathways to it, sure, but not mine
and perhaps not yours.

Mindfulness isn't one size fits all, but it offers an array of
sizes, and there is a fit for all *but* only if you want to wear it.

That's the kicker.

Only if you're seeking it.

Only if you want to pay for it with your time and energy.

Only if you're at a place in your life where you value it.

I repeat: only if you want it, but even more than that,
it has to fit into your life.

I want to be more "mindful;" I really do.

As a thirty-five-year-old mother of three
who wants nothing more than to be

a good woman,

wife,

and an even better mom and human, and even more than
that to raise the best kids into the best kind of adult humans,

I have no doubt I could/would benefit from a balanced
mental state of being fully present and aware of my feelings
and associated actions at all times.

Phew. That was a mouthful.

Still, for now, with the stage I'm in with three under the
age of ten and living through a pandemic, I'm delighted to
accept the notion that having a full mind doesn't mean I'm
not or can't be mindful; it just means that my mind—like my
schedule and house—has a lot going on and is full and that
I'm doing my dang best to handle and appreciate all of it.

It's been said that mindfulness is being aware of what's happening without wishing it were different and enjoying moments as they are. OK. Fine. But I'm going to suggest that if your hot mess self is feeling stressed, not in love with all your moments, but you're still present because you're freakin' there and living through every challenging minute that comes your way, you're plenty mindful.

Saying "No"

Is allowed.

Is encouraged.

Is warranted.

And is hella necessary.

As a semireformed, work-in-progress people pleaser, I
struggle with saying no to people.

When invited somewhere.

When my presence is requested at an event or gathering.

When given unsolicited responsibilities.

When my plate is too full.

When I just don't wanna.

When saying yes would inconvenience me and cause me
anxiety.

But I have every damn right to deliver a negation
if I see fit or so choose.

And that's without an explanation.

Though those are nice and a way to be kind to those you are in essence turning down or turning away, it's not required that you explain yourself or your reasons to anyone.

One thing you do have to remember, though, is that people can and will say no to you, and you've got to remember that there is no expectation for them to offer you an explanation either.

Instead, simply chalk up any "no" you receive to being correctly suited for that person and, therefore, the right choice in the given situation.

Now, when it comes to the love nuggets you birthed and their lack of desire to respond with "yes" to your requests for them to

clean their room,

do their chores,

etc.,

let's remember that while our kids need to respect us and listen to us, and do as they are respectfully, appropriately, and kindly instructed,

they are also allowed to have opinions, and, sometimes, they will be of the opinion of saying no.

Be understanding of them, just like you hope people will be for you.

Social Niceties

They are important.

Inside your home,

at work.

Out in the community.

In car lines.

At the movies.

In restaurants. Holy heck, absolutely in restaurants—
especially as a patron.

At any place of business,

at a bar,

at "Mom's night out."

At the PTA board meeting or on a Zoom conference.

Presenting with good manners, at all times, isn't fake. It's
unconditionally respectful, and that, well, I don't see how it's
anything less than truly admirable and a thoroughly awesome
example to set for your children.

HONESTY

It's hard.

Probably the most challenging is being truthful with ourselves
about all that we are and all that we aren't, our less-than-
admirable traits and negative habits,

and where we could stand to improve.

Beyond owning all that, honesty is hard within a marriage
and keeping open communication with your partner and
about what you need from them.

Being honest with your village, being open
and vulnerable, and willing to say,

"I can't do this alone. I'm struggling today,
and I need your help" is incredibly

ego deflating,

embarrassing

and, for some,

anxiety and guilt provoking.

But to be your authentic self and own worst, keepin'-it-real
critic is vital if you want to grow, change, and have healthier

relationships and a stronger support system.

And can I be honest with you?

You freakin' rock, and you should often remind yourself of that.

LIES

They run rampant.

They are on the loose, and they will chase you down.

The ones we tell ourselves.

The ones filtered social media feeds tell us.

The ones the media itself force-feeds us.

"You can't work and be a good mom."

"You stay home with your kids 'cause
you're lazy and unmotivated."

"You're fat."

"That's too lofty of a dream you have, don't chase it."

"You can't be 'this' unless you are 'that' first."

"You don't do enough."

"You're not strong enough."

"You're not smart enough."

"You're not pretty enough."

"You can't do it."

"You should give up."

"You are not worthy."

All lies.

All stupid AF lies.

Lies so ridiculous they are worthy of this
generally polite-speaking mama's potty mouth.

But we won't say another damn thing about them.

We won't give them any more attention than we already have.

We will scrub all untruths and never let them ever see the
light of the day or come out of our mouths again.

We will pay them no further mind.

Here's something that's not a lie, though…you're a hell of a
human being, and that will never change (even if you do).

ACCEPTANCE

Of all that you are and all that you are not.

Of who you were and who you're becoming.

Of who you raised and who you married.

Of all humans, regardless of

race,

ethnicity,

religion,

gender,

sexual orientation,

size,

appearance,

political affiliation,

beliefs,

or opinions.

When you accept that all any of us has is one very

precious, fast-moving, often hard life and that we're each unconditionally permitted to live ours how we see fit, you'll find more peace than you ever will searching for and living in opposition to that fact.

Being Direct

Never is there a more critical time in a woman's life for her to
be direct with everyone else in hers then when she is riding

the

human female,

wife,

and mother train

all at once.

This shit is hard, and it's always been challenging, especially
in 2020/2021 but absolutely across the decades.

I've only lived for three plus of them, but so far,
the one we're in, it's a kicker.

As in kicking our butts, and by "our," I mean

you,

me,

and every married, child-rearing woman you run into.

So we have to be

clear about our expectations

and downright matter-of-fact about
what's working for us and what is not.

We have to be no-nonsense when it comes
to ensuring we never have an empty cup,
and we need to remember that being (respectfully)
outspoken isn't a character flaw; it's a superpower.

I'm not good at being plainspoken. I never really have been.

But I'm getting better.

Because I'm working at it.

I've realized that I need to be more candid and frank
to be happy, and perhaps the same goes for you.

RISK

From marrying at a young age, just out of college,
to a man eight years my senior to dropping out
of law school after one semester.

To gettin' right on the baby making and raising train and
riding that bad boy for many years, having no idea what I was
doing and how my spouse and I would make it all work.

I'm no stranger to risk.

Even in my younger years, I was a risky little thing,

experimenting with all sorts of hair colors and outfits,

being the only girl playing soccer on the boys' teams,

singing Mariah Carey songs at voice lesson showcases,

and applying to colleges
I just knew I wouldn't get into, like, NYU.

To moving from Florida to Boston, all on my own, and
completing my studies in New England.

Venturing to Acapulco for spring break, drinking too much,
and bungee jumping (not my finest seventy-two hours).

Then moving in with my now husband, then boyfriend while

I was still in college and taking in a chocolate lab puppy
who will forever be our "first baby."

Getting married two months after college graduation,

applying and getting accepted to
and starting law school as a newlywed,

and dropping out of law school
(because what newlywed wants to be doing that?)
without a real plan for what would be next.

To moving again.

And making babies—lots of them—a trio, to be exact, each
about two years apart, and not really knowing what I was in
for and if I would be a good mom.

Since all that, I've started and
maintained a parenting blog and

begun cohosting a podcast with author and positive
psychologist Dr. Robert Zeitlin
(which I'll try to pick back up postpandemic),

and I've written this rambling of a book
you've got here in your hands.

All of what I've done here, folks, I was winging it. With a wish
and a prayer, I went after what I thought was meant for me
and what I wanted.

Taking chances is scary.

Making big decisions is hard.

Risk is, well, you guessed it…risky.

But you know what I don't want to risk?

Letting this one life of mine pass me by and find myself
wishing I hadn't or hungering for a second chance to

throw sh*t against the wall and see what sticks,

get busy chasing dreams,

and let go of fear—of failure or otherwise.

This is our first chance. Our one chance.

So throw caution to the wind when appropriate
(your gut will know when this is and isn't), and remember
that there's nothing worse than not doing what you want
with the life you've got.

FAITH

It isn't one size fits all.

I was

raised Catholic,

married a non-Catholic,

and consider myself a Christian (and a good one).

I had my kids baptized, but I don't go to church,
haven't in years, and nor do my kids go to any sort
of bible study or Sunday school.

But none of that matters, in my opinion anyway, and if yours
is different than mine, that's allowed. I'm OK with it, and you
should be too. 'Cause I belong to the Everyone Is Entitled to
Their Own Opinion Club, but if you're not a member, no
biggie, just skip this part.

To me, faith isn't about dressing myself in a title, aligning
my every word and action with a strict and überrestrictive
religion or pigeonholing myself into what a church
or a crowd of self-described God-loving others say a person
who loves and believes in God and has faith
must look, sound, and act like.

Here's what I believe when it comes to faith as it relates to religion:

I believe in a God.

I believe there is one God.

I believe it's OK for others to have a different perception of who/what "God" is.

I believe there is a higher power at play at all times.

I believe the universe loves me
because I believe the universe loves all of us.

I believe that every human has a responsibility
to be a good person and that, really,
that's all the universe and God desires from us.

Here's what I believe when it comes to faith in its secular,
more social, and personal form:

You've got to keep faith in yourself.

You've got to keep faith in others.

You've got to remember that faith is what keeps your cup full
and your heart and soul full if ever your cup falls empty.

I have faith in you that you'll squeeze something of
importance from my semi-all-over-the-place verbose, and I
have faith in myself that I'll get better at digressing.

Let's see on the next page.

STORIES

Yours matter.

Just as much as the person sitting next to you.

So tell them—your stories.

Tell all of them.

Not just the ones that paint you, your life, and yours in a
beautifully filtered light.

Tell them.

Share why you're awesome and why you suck.

Share your stories with those who love you and with those
who have yet to figure out that they do.

Share your stories of the past and your present-day stories,
and even share with others the story you are telling yourself
will be your future.

Say your shiitake out loud or write it down.

Just get it out of your head and out into the world.

Sharing your stories is good therapy for you, and it's very
likely it's also the exact therapy someone else needs.

Body Size

It sure doesn't correlate a freakin' bit with your worth, you hear me?

Do you believe me?

Do I believe me?

We better.

I've been all over the map when it comes to my weight.

As an out-of-college adult, I have weighed as low as 121 pounds (when I was sick with the flu) and as high as 269 pounds (when I was pregnant with my second child).

For a good while, I hung around 200 pounds, and I've spent quite some time around 170 pounds.

Then,

with the help of a calorie-tracking app,

a butt load of effort,

minimal exercise, but a pretty strict eating regime,

I got myself down to 148 pounds
in about a year's time frame.

Present day, I

moderately exercise,

eat healthy(ish) during the week,

gorge on the weekends,

and live the space between 142 and 148 pounds.

The numbers don't matter, not a dang bit, but the message
does, and I've only shared "my numbers" here to ensure a
vast number of women feel they can relate.

I'd be lying if I told you that I don't

watch what I eat,

stalk my scale,

or very regularly fall victim to the trap that is basing my
beauty and value to this world on my body size and how I
look.

I have a feeling that for most of us,
this will be a forever battle.

So here's what I'm telling myself and you…

We might never win this game, but we can still choose
not to attend or participate in this begrudgingly
self-promoted self-worth contest.

Don't participate in the demise of your self-esteem because

you are trying so hard to meet ridiculous, nonsensical,
ill-placed body standards.

Do, though, participate in life *and meals* and loving and
rocking, now and always, the body you've got—however
much it weighs or jiggles—because, really, it's pretty
impressive when you think about all that it's done
in the years you've been alive.

BALANCE

There's no such thing as "perfect" equilibrium.

You will never feel as though you are balancing appropriately and equally.

You will, without a doubt, be

juggling people and things,

and multitasking,

but the scale will almost always tilt in a particular direction.

Not just that, but one of those balls you've got in the air will almost always fall (or smack you in the face),

and your multitasking will inevitably lead to one, two, or a few mistakes.

So that's why you've got to place only minimal importance on achieving the holy grail of "balance," and instead, focus yourself on making sure you are mentally and emotionally in the best place to willingly and contently keep a steady pace of "doing the best I can."

PAIN

From any incurred during your youth

to any due to loss and grief

to the hurt caused by losing

friendships,

jobs,

and relationships

to the literal pain of childbirth and the daily emotional
trauma you put yourself through
just trying to be a good human,

pain is inescapable.

But…through all that pain…we become more capable.

So there's that.

VALIDATION

I'm not sure why we women, especially us mamas,
seek it so much.

Soliciting it from

our child-rearing peers,

husbands,

kids,

and general society.

Why is it that my hella filtered picture of my #blessed "mom
life" must get at least ten likes for me to feel good about
myself and the often thankless job I'm doing?

That sucks, and so I'm working on it, trying to remember that
I don't need my life choices approved by others, and perhaps
you need to remind yourself of the same.

Here's to neither of us wasting one more minute thinking
that a human outside of ourselves is allowed to approve or
disapprove of us or us even caring about if they do.

FREEDOM

You've got it,

so don't you ever forget it, which can happen easily when you are a parent, and you feel like yours has been stolen from you.

There's freedom

to be who you are,

to raise your kids how you want,

to ignore anyone's expectations for you or your family,

to find fulfillment,

to chase your dreams,

to spend your one life in a way that delivers to you the most fulfillment.

Now go out there and celebrate your freedom by being you, living just as you see fit, and letting the world just stand around in awe of you.

Nothing but the Truth

Living your truth is the only way to live.

Not

your friends',

mom's,

dad's.

Not your sister's.

Not the one any expert tells you to live.

Not the one that a total nonexpert like myself suggests you do
if it doesn't work or feel right for you.

Not anyone's but your own.

And your truth is fluid because remember
that you are not a static being.

You are not a robot.

You are expected and allowed to have a plethora of
personalities (Lord knows I do) and present them

whenever,

however,

and to whom you see fit.

For me, I don't feel like I fully came into my own and began owning my very many truths until I hit the age of thirty.

And every year since I've fallen more in love with who I am and the fact that who that is is constantly changing and transforming.

I sincerely wish you the same level of acceptance and that freeing feeling, and I greatly hope my words are helping you get there.

BEAST MODE

Say hello to "beast mode,"

or don't.

'Cause the very cool thing about your incredibly personal and unique "power mode" is that you (and only you) get to decide when to turn it on and when to power it off.

And your "beast mode" is going to look a lot different from other women you know and your mom friends.

Perhaps in my beast mode, I get six pages written.

But maybe with yours, you bang out a three-course delicious home-cooked meal.

Beast mode for you could just be getting a single load of laundry folded.

Beast mode for me could mean vacuuming and mopping my whole house.

Many things affect our ability and desire to operate at an extraordinary productivity level or sometimes even at an average one.

But remember,

the output does not equal input,

meaning that if all you've done on any given day
is taken said day's challenges and stressors

and are still standing at the end of the day,

you worked hard to get there even if

you didn't get any work done,

fed the kids and yourself McDonald's for dinner, and

left a load of clothes in both the dryer and the washer,

or your home's floor is decorated in pet hair and Legos.

Even if, even then.

Honey, you are a beautiful beast of a human,
so please keep reminding yourself of that.

CHOICE

You have one always—in every moment.

And if ever you make the wrong one,

don't fret—

another opportunity and choice are on the horizon,
and this time, you can make the right one.

Now let all past ones go, and look forward to all those
on the horizon.

EMPOWERED

Know that you are.

Innately.

Thanks to him, your creator, or whomever you believe
helped you to land on this earth.

And thanks to the family that raised you if you were lucky
enough to have a good and supportive one.

And if you weren't, know that you have yourself to thank for
your personally developed awesomeness.

And don't forget to marry someone who makes you feel
this and surround yourself with people and friendships that
regularly remind you of your unwithering capability.

And then be that person for your kids.

Gosh, it feels empowering just to think and talk about
empowerment, doesn't it?

I think so.

LAZY

Let yourself be lazy every once in a while.

On any given day, if you're trending in that direction,
your body, mind, or soul needs the break, so give in to it.

Give it to yourself.

Even if it feels

uncomfortable,

like a cop-out,

or induces guilt.

Do it anyway.

I'll set the example and do it here
by not even finishing this sent…

EXPERTS

There's a lot of them out there, and I'm not one.

Not on

families,

marriage,

self-improvement,

or raising kids.

And surely not on fourth-grade math
(effing fractions and arrays!)

But *you are.*

When it comes to

your family,

marriage,

and kids,

you are the only expert on what you and they need and how
things in and for your nucleus should operate.

Trust your gut always.

LEADERSHIP

As the matriarch of your little (or big) nuclear cohort,
whether you like it or not, you are the captain of the ship and
in charge of making sure it doesn't go down.

It's your responsibility to keep your people safe, bring 'em
morally up right, and deliver to the world some fully grown,
respectful, and well-raised cargo.

You are the train conductor and its engineer.

You are the pilot and its hardworking crew.

You are so much to those you brought into this world, and
now it's your intrinsically established directive to guide them
to a happy, fulfilling, and meaningful life.

And sometimes it's hard to lead people when we

don't have a map or

the best sense of direction

or feel qualified enough to navigate anyone else through this
life, let alone ourselves.

But hard is good for us.

It's good for you, it's good for me, and it's also great for the

people we lead because the best kind of leaders,
in my opinion, are the ones who are

figuring it out as they go,

adaptable,

and open and ready to receive this world and its adventures
for what they are and as they come.

You're a terrific example for your kid because you just keep
going no matter the weather you face, and that's why it's
wonderful you're the face they follow.

The Need for Speed

Is a fallacy, one I've found myself hitched to.

And maybe the same goes for you.

Things can be done slow, and just because something doesn't happen right away doesn't mean it's not meant for you.

Just because a change you are trying to implement, for yourself or as a family, isn't accepted with open arms or easily adapted to doesn't mean it can't ever happen.

And just because it's taking a while to climb that promotion ladder at work, it doesn't mean you're not "cut out" for the position or that you should give up.

You know, when I was a kid, my parents dubbed me Speedy Gonzales because of how fast I moved around and spoke and how quickly I would get bored with something and start rushing onto the next thing.

And also how quickly I wanted things to happen.

I haven't really rid myself of that
"gotta go, gotta go right now" nature.

But it's taken a patient, slower-moving, every-moment-loving husband and putting-up-with-me kids for me to figure out that no, the early bird doesn't always get the worm and that

sometimes the early bird is so freakin' early
that the worm is not even there yet.

So while yes, there is something to be said for being a
"go-getter," even the "slightly slower-to-get-going go-getters"
get to where they wanna go, and honestly,
they're probably less grumpy about the ride
because they took their time and tried to enjoy it.

MOMMY, I NEED YOU

I always thought I'd never get tired of hearing that.

That I'd be the kind of parent and woman who would always—for every draining second of every child-raising minute of my days—feel grateful for my family and truly honored to be needed so much.

Spoiler alert: I'm not her.

I'm grateful, yes.

Honored? Most definitely.

But do I feel that way every second? Hell to the no.

Some days I'm overtouched, overneeded,
and plain and simply "over it."

Some days "Mommy, I need you" feels like too much.

But do you know what gets me through those kinds of days?

Knowing that the years of my kids not just needing me but wanting me so incessantly are fleeting.

It's a lot to have one, two, three, or any number of children depending on you to be their forever lifeline, and forever you sure will be.

It's a lot of work to be at their beck and call. But by doing that now and responding to their overload of requests for your

presence,

affection,

attention

and love,

it's how you raise

successfully independent,

appropriately attached,

well-loved humans,

and, honestly,

the world can never have too many of these.

Child: "Mommy, I need you."

Mommy: "I'm on my way, child."

I'm doing this for them.

I'm doing this for me.

I'm doing this for you.

You're welcome, world.

LABOR

From the work you put in to get yourself through school

to the jobs you've worked to get where you are now

to the work you've put into friendships, relationships,
and perhaps a marriage

to the actual laboring of those sweet babies of yours.

To the emotional and physical labor it takes
to raise littles into bigs,

there's no question that you've been giving so much
of yourself to this world for a long time.

Please, please, please heed this:

make sure that you put the same damn incredible effort
you've been putting into living

into loving yourself *always*.

And I want you to know this…

This book has been a labor of love for me,
and I hope that you've enjoyed it and will continue to.

You know, my favorite kind of self-improvement,

motherhood, parenting-centered books are the kinds
that deliver pockets of practical wisdom in small,
quick-to-read, easy-to-digest doses, and I hope that
I have done that for you here.

I hope that if ever the labor of loving yourself or others feels
like "too much," you come back here, to me. To this book. To
these words. And that you find that glimmer of inspiration or
hope you (and so very many of us) very often dearly need.

In Closing

You know, this whole book has kind of been like one of those games where you are given a word and you say the first thing that comes to your mind when you hear that word or topic— that's what I've been doing. Giving my off-the-cuff take on everything that comes to mind on these matters as they relate to me as a woman, wife, and mom.

I'm not a sage.

On parenting or anything.

I think I've made that clear, and who am I kidding? I'm positive that's got to be totally apparent.

All this book has been,

all it will ever be,

is me passing along what I think are insightful or at least thought-provoking ramblings on many of the things we deal with as women and mothers.

And while I pray to God that this book does

something,

anything

positive for you

—even if it just serves as a coloring book for your child (yay! I'm happy I can keep them busy) or a drink coaster for you (sip, sip, hooray!)—

I'm proud of it.

Because just as with motherhood, I went into writing having no clue what I was doing. But the therapy of writing, and the therapy of birthing and raising minis who mirror the human I am, has done more for me than I ever could have imagined.

Here's hoping this book did more for you than I could have ever imaged and that it delivers to you exactly what you need when you need it.

Now go love well yourself and that incredible family of yours, you badass woman.

I'm always on your side.

ABOUT THE AUTHOR

Nicole Merritt is a mother of three, a freelance writer, co-host of *I am the Worst Parent Ever Podcast*, and the Owner and Founder of *jthreeNMe*, an imperfectly authentic peek at real-life marriage, parenting, and self-improvement. *jthreeNMe* is raw, honest, empowering, inspiring, and entertaining; it's like chicken soup for parents who are exhausted, over-worked, over-stressed, and under-inebriated, yet still utterly happy. Nicole's work is regularly featured by NBCUniversal's the TODAY SHOW and TODAY PARENTS, where her readership is over 1.5 million. Nicole's words have also been published by Love What Matters, Scary Mommy, That's Inappropriate, Ravishly, The Good Men Project, Elephant Journal, CafeMom, Popsugar, Grown and Flown, Working Mother Magazine, BLUNTmoms, Thought Catalog, Everyday Family,  Motherly, Sammiches & Psych Meds, Red Tricycle & others. Nicole's a law school dropout who wants people to know that they can do any goshdarn thing they put their mind to, and all of her words are intended to remind you (and her) of such.

Made in the USA
Columbia, SC
25 July 2021